PROVINCETOWN POETS SERIES
first books by new poets

VOLUME VII
David Matias
Fifth Season

VOLUME VI
Ellen Dudley
Slow Burn

VOLUME V
Mairym Cruz-Bernal
On Her Face the Light of La Luna

VOLUME IV
Martha Rhodes
At the Gate

VOLUME III
Anne-Marie Levine
Euphorbia

VOLUME II
Michael Klein
1990

VOLUME I
Keith Althaus
Rival Heavens

AT THE GATE

PROVINCETOWN POETS, VOLUME IV
Series Editor: Christopher Busa

AT THE GATE

by Martha Rhodes

PROVINCETOWN ARTS PRESS

ACKNOWLEDGMENTS

Grateful acknowledgment is made to the following periodicals where some of these poems, at times in earlier versions, first appeared:

Beloit Poetry Journal: "Dreaming of Flight," "Inside Father's Pockets," "Who Knew"

Bomb Magazine: "Our Bedroom Wall," "These Are the Nights"

The Cape Rock: "Inheriting My Sister," "Without It"

The Florida Review: "Fall Visit," "Her Future," "In the Sick Room," "Like Today"

The Global City Review: "Neither of Us"

The Jacaranda Review: "The Robe"

Ploughshares: "Possession"

Provincetown Arts: "The Nude"

Quarterly West: "Infestation"

The Virginia Quarterly Review: "All The Soups," "Recurrent Fever," "Soft Rag," "Song," "Sweeping the Floor"

I am forever grateful to Jean Alain Brunel whose love and companionship have facilitated the writing of these and subsequent poems.

My deepest gratitude to the following writers, my teachers and friends, for their generous responses to the poems: Joan Aleshire, Jane Brox, Lynn Emanuel, Dzvinia Orlowsky, Marcia Pelletiere, Michael Ryan, John Skoyles, and Ellen Bryant Voigt. For their encouragement, I thank these writers: Ruth Anderson Barnett, Marietta Whittlesey Berkey, Peter Josyph, Pat Mangan, D. Nurkse, Alethea Gail Segal; and my sisters, Karen Rhodes Clarke and Paula Rhodes Vannelli.

I wish to thank the MacDowell Colony and the Millay Colony for the Arts where some of these poems were written during residencies.

This book is funded in part by the Massachusetts Cultural Council, a state agency that also receives support from the National Endowment for the Arts. Additional support has been provided by contributions from foundations, corporations, and individuals.

Published by PROVINCETOWN ARTS PRESS, INC.
650 Commercial Street, Provincetown, MA 02657

FIRST EDITION – 2ND PRINTING 1999

Designed by Gillian Drake
Frontispiece by Richard Baker

PAPER ISBN: 0-944854-18-4
CLOTH ISBN: 0-944854-19-2

Library of Congress Catalog Card Number: 94-73949

PRINTED IN USA

For Katherine Titus

CONTENTS

I

Recluse   5

For Her Children   6

Often the Children   7

Recurrent Fever   8

Family Pond   9

My Mother's Map   10

Infestation   11

When You, a Puppy   12

The Nude   13

The Robe   14

Garden Cat   15

Our Bedroom Wall   16

Behind Me   17

Possession   18

In They Go   19

Why She Hurries Out, Then Home   20

In the Sick Room   21

II

Orbits: A Sequence

Orbits   25

Bare Windows   26

Days Off   27

Inside Father's Pockets   28

All the Soups   29

Dreaming of Flight   30

Into the Fens   31

These Are the Nights   32

Song   33

Who Knew   34

Like Today   35
A Small Pain   36
Fall Visit   37
Her Future   38
His   39
Soft Rag   40

I I I

Out of Father's Wallet   43
Till Eight   44
For Once   45
Without It   46
Anniversary   47
Neither of Us   48
Telling Mother About My Troubled Marriage   49
Little Ditch in My Kitchen   50
Across the Lawn   51
Inheriting My Sister   52
Quarantine   53
Dry   54
Sweeping the Floor   55
I Turned, No Longer Needing   56
Raft   57

AT THE GATE

I

RECLUSE

She wanders room to room.
There are two sofas, two places to lie,

there are four chairs, four places to sit,
there's a desk and table

and a cat in different moods. There are books
too easy and too hard to read,

inherited vases she won't touch,
clothes on the floor she kicks into corners,

food she wants but the store's too far,
a bed for two that's now used to one,

an old clock too fast or too slow,
a bulb burnt out and none to replace it,

one body to soothe but the body says no.

FOR HER CHILDREN

She pretends to be dead
and unless you creep up and pinch her someplace tender
you think she really is dead.

Then she gets up—
refreshed now, pink-cheeked,
her hair a little sweaty.

Those short bursts of lightness after sleep—
the noiseless house, bright and aired,
the children butterflies,
delighted when she scoops them up in her net.

For them, she does not move
and they must not wake her
and they must not pinch her ever again.

OFTEN THE CHILDREN

Often the children, returning
from restaurant, movie, or beach,
sleep in the back of the car.

Up the driveway, past crickets
and half-killed birds, they're carried
quickly to their separate rooms.

But the house creaks,
too much noise for the youngest.
Her floor is noisy,

her ceiling has shapes on it.
The crab apple tree will unlock the screen
if she opens her eyes,

will swallow her pillows.
But if she lies face down
and makes herself sleep,

it hides in shadows with the other sheep.

RECURRENT FEVER

Whose room is this?
What lucky soul's bedroom has a lake
deep as my closet
and a bed canopied by a willow tree?
I like sleeping in shade.
Mother's hand on my forehead is a blessing,
no malice in my heart.

Pneumonia, pneumonia, just what I dreamed,
like when I was little and wouldn't breathe.
Everyone circled over my sheets.
She had 3 heads. She had none.
I wouldn't see straight for a week.

The cats are fighting. Mama Cat's
climbing the willow, she's dripping milk.
He's biting their necks.
Will Papa Cat eat the kittens?
Will he drop them in the lake?
Can he open the closet door with his little paw?
Three in a basket. Is she carrying them away?

FAMILY POND

in memory of Lucy Bradshaw Cannatella

The family pond where Lucy drowned is only
eight feet deep. She swam there every summer day
every summer of her life. That morning
her daughter, sunning naked on the halfway raft,
saw too late it wasn't a game:
her brother sliding down her mother's back
(he was found blue, bloated, but alive),
their two heads bobbing half a dozen times.
Now where are they? What's taking so long?
She clings to the little dock, waiting to be rocked,
kicking at the dark ripples and bubbles.
They're down there plotting
just an arm's length below.

MY MOTHER'S MAP

Behind the door,
under the bed,
under the floor
and inside the boiler—
seeping into the vault, below
the sidewalk, through sewers
and sludge, granite and foundations,
through lava pools and undersea craters
and past where she used to think
China was—below and through dark spaces
into whirls and halos of gases,
icicles of light, past time and into time again—
through reflections of past and reflections
of present, my mother travels almost every day.

I hold out my hand and she draws her map
so I'll always know where she is.

INFESTATION

Which of them had the idea
to write my name on an envelope,
seal itself in
and slip under my door at dinner time?

Who will kill them for me,
string them for a necklace,
weave their milky eyes
through the branches of my tree
so others will know not to come?

Who will chase them with brooms,
stamp them under boots,
glue them to paper,
shovel them, shake them from logs,
listen at wallboards for more?

The clothes I wear, gray thick shadows
buttoned past my neck, even in summer, aren't enough
when the field is blacked out and all wires down,
when they're lined up on my hearth
and the house is teeming.

WHEN YOU, A PUPPY

The dog you know you are has mange.
Incurable, since you lick and scratch.
Your owner considers a bath. But you refuse,
remembering that last one, with her sister,
when you, a puppy,
loved all water, loved
learning the dog paddle.

You'll never forget, will you,
the sister kneeing you down
till you bit and bit her hand,
that leg, and bubbles swirled pink
and her father, disgusted, tore you away.
Just look at you,

oh, look at you,
still shivering in the corner.

THE NUDE

When I lay for three-hour stretches
on his torn, gold velvet pillows
refusing both coffee and toilet,
I was eighteen and did not consider other jobs.

The ritual of undressing, our ritual,
his back turned, and me unbuttoned,
unbraiding my hair, bent over
and shaking it loose, did not bring us closer.

He never watched, only whispered,
May we begin?
And my answer was the creak of his sofa.

Now I am here, in this gallery,
fifteen years younger and still looking
past him to his wife posed at the piano,
her photo on the table behind him, that photo

always with us, even on the day he startled me,
his hand on my ankle and told me
our work together was finished.
It wasn't finished.

I knew nothing about her artist/husband.
But I could make up anything,
and even if it took me years,
I would write and tell her everything.

THE ROBE

After his shower he reaches for
her robe, not the sexless terry
but the white satin down to the floor.
And she imagines softness and curves on him
as he walks around the kitchen,
drinks his coffee, bends to pet the cat,
reaches for more sugar, bends again,
wiping what he's spilled from her foot.

How will she love him like this, should she
pull him by the sash to bed
or bare his shoulders, oil him first
then slowly rub him dry with her palms?
Where are the breasts and wide hips
she thought she saw? What do they want
each other to want—both of them
standing here shy.

GARDEN CAT

I closed the door once—
now I leave it open.
He does not let me touch him.
Inside, he eats in the corner I chose
for him, warm behind the kindling.
We have never been closer
than across the room. At night
when you turn to me,
my arms cross my chest.
You unfold and hold them down,
licking me quietly, whispering.
It's been years like this together.

OUR BEDROOM WALL

Why do I always let you die,
not lifting you from bed, just watching you
lie breathless as your spirit
dangles from our bedroom wall
till it gives up and it's dead too.
Poof, I dream, no more you.

Why do I sit in our quiet room,
wet from the shower, while our cats
lick my legs dry and the morning light
throws our neighbor out of his bath
and onto our wall. Smash that man,
he's dead too. You see,
it's not just you.

Even people I've never held
fall ill or drown or fold in half.
My red sad dreams cover our wall,
dreams that kill us all.

BEHIND ME

I think he was behind me.
I think he wore a hat.
I think I ran inside a store
and asked if I could wait.

I think I called my husband.
I think he was asleep.
I know he didn't hear the phone
that rang till I gave up.

I think he was behind me.
I think he grabbed my arm.
I know a car door opened next
and then he disappeared.

I think I took a shower.
I think I saw a bruise.
I think my husband was asleep.
I think he wore a hat.

POSSESSION

Steal big sister's presents.
Swallow pieces,
ride her bike, ride it far
into the grove.

Show her you've discovered
all her holy spots

and watch her try to find another,
deeper forest. Everything she's kept from you
is yours now: these frilly private things,
this tiny book of screams.

IN THEY GO

I'm burying our daughter
next to her brother, both
children I've always dreamed
looked like you.
I'm tucking them in,
covering their sleep for the last time.

It's dangerous for you here,
thousands of microscopic graves
packed with pacifiers and trucks.
Even jumpers and jackets
still on store racks.
In they go, hangers and all.

Don't stare at me.
Don't tell me I go too far.
I can make graves for days.

She's always expecting disaster,
blood scribbled on walls,
an empty carcass hung from a lamp,
roof and bricks collapsed, all she owns
shredded and burnt.
                    Watching others' children
on their way to school,
stiff in their snowsuits,
reach to hug their parents goodbye,

she hurries out, then home,
counts the blocks, forces her hands
in her pockets (everyone's safe, she is safe).

She's always resisting what's criminal in her,
a small gray cloud waiting at the gate.

IN THE SICK ROOM

Fetal under covers,
I sensed the day's progression
by the sounds of high-pitched
French classes one hall over,
the smell of Miss Milton's
formaldehyde, and scufflings
of flats, field hockey cleats
and blue Pappagallo pumps.
Alone in the sick room
and finally forgotten,
I imagined my mother
at home, stiff on the sofa,
hair shorter on one side,
garden scissors in her lap.
New lies every day, every day
makeup smeared across her face,
our half-dried wash on the floor,
recipes and ads cut out into trees.
I thought of my room,
how she'd forget I was gone
and look for me, tossing
my bed upside down, puzzles
into corners. There I was
at school, curled up in my cot,
unable to touch
the nape of her freckled neck,
to fold her scented tissue
into a square, dry her eyes,
then turn it over
and dry her eyes again.

II

ORBITS

a sequence

ORBITS

tramp tramp to Boston
tramp tramp to town
watch out little girl
or you'll fall down
　　　　　—nursery rhyme

Tramping me to Boston on your knees,
my heels on your shoulders—how easy it was
shooting me all the way to the North Pole,
to the very top of our frigidaire
where I was the coldest,
most remote person in the world.
Or lifting me to kiss the warm round bulbs
in the ceiling, watching me lick each star goodnight—
do you remember our orbits around the universe,
the small and large circles we journeyed
together, alone in our little house?

BARE WINDOWS

There weren't any curtains in my parents' house,
not while we lived there. Who's there now,
who drapes the windows on every floor
so no one can look through anymore?

I drive slowly past expecting to see
Father in the hedges creeping underneath,
under my window, pretending to weed.
It's Saturday. I'm sleeping.

Mother wanted curtains but he said No.
He built this house, he did, not her,
and he demanded windows that stay bare.
So wherever I dressed I crept down low.
Even now, away from there.

DAYS OFF

Whoever planted this garden wanted no one
to see in. That's what I noticed first,
the high wooden fence, the height of trees.

My father dragged me across our field,
mowing and chopping all the unwanted things.
It was work making a lawn green.
Poison ivy burned in heaps.

Who planted this garden?
Who wanted who not to see in?

Mother sleeps all day, no matter what.
I run through the sprinkler, in and out,
my madras shorts streaking
my legs, purple and red.

It was work keeping our new lawn green,
work getting my body clean.

INSIDE FATHER'S POCKETS

I was sticking my hands into his pockets,
changing jacks for quarters
and spitting one wet marble
into each shirt pocket
so he'd look like a woman.
I was making him nervous.
He sat me on the couch across the room.
I climbed down twice.
When he carried me to bed,
ordering me to sleep, I lifted
for a kiss, my arms
around his neck and pulled him down
and pulled him down. He breathes,
You always want more, don't you?

Don't I.

ALL THE SOUPS

All the soups I've made in my life—
slow-cooking easy broths, red thick
puréed blends. Churning it all up
alone in my kitchen, tasting,
covering, uncovering, remembering
spat-out carrots pinched between Mother's fingers
and pressed back into my mouth, Mother
wanting to get done with those meals, running
upstairs before Father comes home, Father
grubbing through drawers looking for pints,
both sisters up in the field getting plastered
and laid, me stuck in that chair,
locked behind a metal tray, not knowing
who's slamming the screen door so hard
that waves in my milk cup spill to my lap.
There's always a pot of soup on the stove.
I trace cats and houses on the damp kitchen wall,
waiting for anyone to come home,
waiting for one person
hungry enough to come home.

DREAMING OF FLIGHT

I thought she was dead. Father buried Flight.
But there she is in the corner of my dream,
vicious as the day she ate my rabbits.
I thought she was dead. Father buried Flight,
dragging her past the empty rabbit hut,
then rinsed his bloody shirt in the muddy stream.
I thought she was dead. Father buried Flight.
But here we are in the corner of my dream.

INTO THE FENS

My mother at the kitchen sink
My father at the goldfish tank
My sister on the treehouse roof
winking at the neighbor's boy

My cat and I go hunting for gnats
into the fens clucking our tongues

My mother boils the freezer's ice
My father hangs his shoes to dry
My sister's outside playing mouse
with the neighbor's oldest boy

We're licking our jaws
dry as a squeak

My sister swallows the neighbor's boy
My father plasters the treehouse shut
My mother unmakes all the beds
folding herself into the sheets

THESE ARE THE NIGHTS

These are the nights
I'm nobody's wife.
My nightgown won't lift.

I'll try if you want
but I don't think
I can even bend

or sit in your lap.
Who are you mister who
let you in?

My mother's gone out
locked up the house
keys in her purse.

How long will it take
if I say yes and what'll I get?
If I say nothing, just stand

here like this
can you still do
what you said you'd do

here, lift up my nightgown,
help me lie down.

SONG

I've often seen
my father dead, under a sheet
that's how I've seen
my father dead, that's how I've been
wet in his breath, sailing in blood.

I've often seen
my father's grave, often at night
that's when I've seen
the muddy pit, but could not lean
over his grave, sinking in mud.

I've often seen
our twisted legs, only at night
that's when I've been
buried by him, that's when I've seen
him weep in me, deep in his child.

I've often seen
my father dead, tangled in sheets
that's how I've dreamed
this blood wet dream, a twisted dream
where we're both dead, father and child.

WHO KNEW

She was crying in the kitchen.
I didn't want breakfast.
She hadn't made breakfast,
just a half-frozen lump of juice
in my glass and a spoon.
"He's cheating on me."
I knew and knew with whom.

What dishes would break,
what pills would she take,
why would she write such a long note
then snip it and snip it
into the kitchen pail?
I drank the juice and ran to school.

Tire marks through my hopscotch grid,
all the doors unlocked, she'd left
my two suitcases unpacked,
untouched under my bed.
Who knew when she'd be back?
Who cared if she was dead.

She called when he got home,
when I was in my room,
her letter, pages of blurry tears
pasted together in my drawer,
his voice, a drunken palm
begging at my door.

LIKE TODAY

That evening, drunk in a long black dress
of Mother's and wearing her double strand pearls
and amethyst pin she pierced through my bra strap
so I wouldn't lose it when I rubbed
against whichever young man might choose me,
my hair up and twisted, those black suede spikes,
that night, on the Longwood dance floor,
before I staggered to the ladies' room,
I knew someday I'd end my life in a chair refusing
to walk, not caring when friends tired of me.

I stripped in the white tiled stall not wanting
any man ever in my life, not wanting to touch,
just wanting to feel my nails cut flesh,
watch blood well up from the ten burning
rips across my chest. I'd sit
for however long it takes
to die, like today I'm sitting, while my cat,
fifteen and nearly blind, lies pathetic
by her bowl, empty since morning,
unable to feed herself.

A SMALL PAIN

It's true she liked it.
Mostly when it hurt, a little.
Just a little made it good.
And still does. It's better
if it hurts just a little bit.

So when she buys jeans, they're tight
and she feels their tightness everywhere.
Just a little tight, a small pain.

And when her forehead's hot,
her throat sore, she smokes more cigarettes.
When the soles of her shoes wear thin,
she wears them another season,
till the dents in her heels from the little nail heads
grow hard and red. And when her husband stops talking,
stops holding her hand and tickling her thigh,
stops coming home every night, stops calling her,
stops stopping by, she stays, she stays.
It is winter. The boiler just broke, the blankets
have fallen off the bed. She stays
until she gets a little colder,
just a little colder.

FALL VISIT

He's sweating, his shirt is wet,
the seat of his pants muddy.
So are his hands. He's been digging
since morning, each fall
fifty new tulips and fifty new jonquils.
I have to go out there now.

Mother's saying go out there now.
I have to pat him on his shoulder,
help him up, let him kiss me
wherever his lips catch my face.
Will I ever be able to stand still
and shut my eyes so it'll be over in a second?

No, and his kisses are muddy
wet smears that never rub off.
If I don't go out there now, he'll come
when I'm unpacking or taking a nap.
He will and my room is still so small.

HER FUTURE

When the father holds his daughter
for the first time, folding back
the receiving sheet and balancing
all that she will ever be in his two palms,
can he wait to carry her home
to the rooms he's built himself,
does he think about her future
with him, how he'll start with her toes,
then her thighs, then her still
untender breasts? At the hospital,
does he think it then or slowly
over years, without thought, does it just happen
again and again her body
hushed between his palms?

HIS

He finds the dusty gin,
pours a double, straight,
then another. Lunch will be fast.
He'll sleep after, there,
on the sofa. I'll watch him.

It's mostly my mouth that's his,
and my hair, thinning,
pushing back from my brow, exposing
me, like him.

Oh, I've known since I was seven,
since then I've known I was him,
his.

SOFT RAG

Seventy-three years ago he lay belly up
on the rented bearskin rug, stared at the penny
stuck on his mama's nose, and screeched.

He used to hang beside the bed in my first apartment
until one boyfriend complained,
"Your father's giving me the creeps."

We ceremoniously put him away.

Today I want him between the bookshelves
and my desk. I want him there now,
his lacy dress barely hiding the parts of him

I'm almost forgetting. I pass my hand
in front of his eyes. I spit on the glass
and wipe his body clean with a soft rag.

III

OUT OF FATHER'S WALLET

I'd left her in his wallet long enough,
stared at and thumbed, her tanksuit torn,
and all the children around her
happier, jumping into the lake,
showing off in front of their parents
what they'd learned all summer,
while she crouched on the pier,
blue, cold, always frightened.

It surprised her, asleep in that dark,
when I tore her loose, tossed her into the air.
Now she knows how her friends that summer felt
running, jumping, diving away
for the first time.

TILL EIGHT

Though I don't have children,
I set the table anyway, spooning out
peas, potatoes, and small slices of roast.
I sit at the head chair, eat my portion,
then move to the next and the next,
till all the plates are almost empty—
some children don't like peas, others hate potatoes.

Anyone for dessert?
We can sit on the floor, eat our cookies,
watch TV, and play with Daddy's compass.
He won't be home till eight.
There's plenty of time to clear the table.

FOR ONCE

I hate to be touched, he said,
and this was news to me.

You love to be touched, I said.

No, I hate it.

You mean you hate this? This?
And this?

No . . .

Then what are you talking about?
Be precise.

I just wanted to give him an hour,
his eyes masked, his skin oiled in lavender,
allowing him, for once, to do nothing,
respond
or not,
sleep or drift
so when he said No, I still tried
and when he turned away,
I shoved the sheets off,
was going to get up,
go out,
slam the door.

But he caught my arm
and eased me down.

You love to be touched, he said.
You love this
and this
and this.

WITHOUT IT

My husband doesn't mind how I look
and likes, even, at night
or in the morning, the softness
and warmth, the way my breasts and tummy
move slowly under and around him.

When he says it's painful
to see me rise from a chair, he remembers me
running so easily across the street,
against the lights, and settling
comfortably in the movie theater
into any small seat I now avoid.

Lose it, he says,
for your health, your heart, your life.
But without it, all of it, the wind
lifts my dress and everyone sees
my bones splintering, breaking,
unable to hold me.

ANNIVERSARY

Behind an Indian spread and candlelit,
the tub in our East Seventh kitchen
(missing a leg and poorly caulked)
was wonderfully small,
painted a pale rose and scented
with peach and almond oils.
And down the hall flutes played potions
in our room. One of us would rinse
then run to bed, while the other stayed
till the water ran cold
and the pink splotches of skin faded—
till the other called and called.
Today, all day I prepare for you,
perfuming my kimono,
opening and closing pores,
changing everyday sheets to silks:
not a job, but not love either.

NEITHER OF US

This is not where I thought I'd live, is not
that ramshackle Victorian on Elm Street,
its front steps propped up since neither of us is handy,
its garage filled with tulip bulbs and tires,
its first, second, and third floors wainscotted
and smelling of must. And you're not the husband
I ever imagined having, not the lanky,
absent-minded man who loves children but sometimes
forgets to pick them up from their games,
who'd happily play touch in the yard
if he could see the ball, not the occasionally
tipsy but forever tenured musicologist
who's been working on his symphony for twenty years.
This is not that house, we are not the couple I had in mind.
I saw them today

as I drove down their street. He was raking,
she bagging leaves while their three- and five-year-olds
rode circles around them trying to get them to stop.
He seemed to complain about his blisters,
holding his palms to her face. I sped up,
self-conscious and afraid, the same peculiar woman
driving by month after month.

Back home, I'd rather not tell you where I've been.
Quietly, I take off my coat.
I open a screen, lean out and wave.
Does anyone drive slowly down our street
to stare up at our lace-lit windows?
I'm waving at parked cars, a grocery stand, the bus stop.
Here we are. Who out there
wants to be us?

TELLING MOTHER ABOUT
MY TROUBLED MARRIAGE

How I fell off my bike when I was five
is obvious. I wasn't looking.
Neither were you. We'd just minutes before
taken my training wheels off and this first ride
cost me three teeth two years early.
When my chin exploded on the stone wall,
you were out cold in your bedroom, leaving me
to pull the forsythia branch out of my arm.

Now you're telling me, Honey
there are worse things than being hurt.
Being dead is one, you say,
you who've never seen your daughter bleed.

LITTLE DITCH IN MY KITCHEN,

when they dug I expected to find a body under,
not broken pipes and a mile of river sand
heaving linoleum.

Comforting,
four men working while I wait in my room,
shielded from hammer spray.
Should I offer them lunch—admire their snapshots
of wives and kids in the pool, a doberman
stealing steak from the spit—
or would they prefer the front stoop?

A life so quiet,
when they cover you
I'm alone again.

ACROSS THE LAWN

Mother drives across the lawn
thinking she's out west, suddenly
in Redwood Forest, her forsythia
a grove, Father's stone wall an unexpected
canyon. She drives onto the Hills' lawn,
Mr. and Mrs. Hill waving so she'll miss their pool,
while Father reaches the police on the telephone,
then ambulance, then my sister smoking pot in Boston,
unable to drive straight down any lane herself.
She's higher than usual when he calls (her boyfriend
dumped her yesterday for good; she can't
get out of bed), but this sounds serious,
a psychotic event!

"Mom's gone mad, completely loony,"
her message plays on my machine.
"But don't come down. I'll handle it alone.
I've already made up my sofa for Dad."

I can hear them there, chewing meringues—
tomorrow she'll drive him back to the house,
he'll patch up the wall, pull out those shrubs,
plant them out back where they'll border the swamp,
which he meant to do years ago.

INHERITING MY SISTER

I sit in the rocker
watching you sleep, forty-
year-old thumb pressing
against your teeth.

You pulled the phone
into your bathroom for me to hear
the warm water rise past your neck,
red water on the black and white tiles.

You're not my daughter.
I want you out.
I send you back
as far as our parents' grave,
where they turned you over to me,
where I lifted you, brushed you,
unbuttoned my coat, letting you in.

QUARANTINE

Summer is a mountain
blazing through cornfields
and this house is on fire
but never burns. Mother's wedding china
bakes in the cabinets and in the attic
squirrel food roasts, the nutty smell
settling on my scalp. Under the eaves
sheets peel off my bed like onion skins.

Finally I can sleep, in this kettle,
the lid closed, in the same bed
where so many mornings I've wakened
damp with my family around me.

Now in this fevered light
I paint an X across the door.
I'll sleep through these summer months alone.

DRY

I dream my friend won't die.
The water in her lungs is air.
I'm on her chest, my mouth
in her mouth, dry inside her,
pond water spat in the sand.

In this dream my friend won't die.
Tomorrow she's thirty-five, opening
presents, blowing out candles—her husband
and children, all of us blowing,
filling balloons, breathing air, air,
the pond water dry in the pond.

SWEEPING THE FLOOR

She loves especially the Cha Cha Cha,
her right foot crossing her left
in a daring twist. And sometimes
she tangos wall to wall across the room.
This makes her laugh.

She knows she isn't graceful.
She shuts her eyes to mirrors
and any shiny surface. Years ago,
at a cousin's wedding, someone whispered
in her ear, Dancing with you,
my God, dancing with you,
is like pushing around a piano.

And sometimes when she's dancing fast,
can barely stop, doesn't want to stop,
can't catch her breath, feels very hot,
she gives herself a hug, a squeeze,
a spin, a dip so low her hair,
her short wispy hair seems to brush the floor,
it glides on the floor, it sweeps the floor.

I TURNED, NO LONGER NEEDING

This young cat,
gray and buff, is everything to me.
And so I've hated her, even while my hand,
safe inside a potholder, wrestles, lets her
kick with her back paws, claw with her front,
her bites padded but fierce.

I've thought about starving her,
eating pounds of meat
in front of her,
or over months, inch by inch,
slowly withdrawing my hand
so we just live together,
never touching.

But last night,
ten months without you,
suddenly I turned,
no longer needing both sides
of the bed, nor the phone,
silent on your pillow,
its haunting night light.

She is why,
my young, eager cat
who gently taps my face,
nuzzles under blankets,
the bed warm now,
two of us waking, sleeping.

RAFT

It is a single, cot-sized
slab of foam she's found
while remains from her
household float deeper
into the fens, the Charles'
weakest finger pulling steadily
at the people who once slept upstairs,
now bloated with mud, their air pipes
stopped by bottle caps and doll heads.
Why didn't they wake, as did she,
dragging the mattress
from den through tool room,
to this cinderblock hideaway
under the cellar stairs—
this raft, supporting her body.

COLOPHON

This book was set in Schneidler, printed on acid-free
Mohawk Superfine paper, and bound with a Strathmore
wrapper. The letterpress label was printed by Paul Mendes
Specialty Printing of Provincetown and glued by hand to
the wrapper.

Thirteen hundred and fifty copies were printed for a paper
edition.

One hundred and fifty copies were hardbound with a
tipped-in monoprint by Richard Baker.

The hardbound copies are numbered and signed by
the author and the artist.